In Lou of Going Out

A Collection of Recipes from

Family and Friends

Inspired by Home Cooking during the
COVID-19 Stay-at-Home Effort

Louis J. McNerney

Fulton Books, Inc.
Meadville, PA

Published by Fulton Books 2021

ISBN 978-1-64952-545-1 (paperback)
ISBN 978-1-63710-606-8 (hardcover)
ISBN 978-1-64952-546-8 (digital)

Printed in the United States of America

Contents

Home Chef Contributors' Profiles 5

Appetizers
Spring Rolls 8
Game Day Appetizer 9
Avocado Cilantro Deviled Eggs 10
Spinach Balls 11
Crab Quesadillas with Mango Salsa 12
Artichoke Heart Dip 14
Cajun Crab Cakes 15
Olive Tapenade 17

Soups
Chilled Moroccan Tomato Soup 20
Coconut Squash Soup 21

Salads
Mandarin Superfoods Salad 24
Watermelon Goat Cheese Salad 25
Asparagus and Tomato Salad with Yogurt Dressing 26
Zesty Mediterranean Salad 27
Pesto Orzo with Sun-Dried Tomato 28

Breakfast
Easy Sausage Quiche 30
Sausage and Pepper Frittata 31

Mains
Fusilli with Lemon Cream Sauce, Shrimp, and Spinach 34
Pan-Seared Salmon with Lemon Butter Cream Sauce 36
Steamed Halibut in Lettuce Leaves 37
Rigatoni Bolognese 40
Tandoori Chicken Skewers 41
Grilled Hawaiian Style Chicken Skewers 43
Slow Roasted Chicken (Fall off the Bone Juicy) 44
Roast Beef Tenderloin 45
Lemon Spaghetti with Shrimp 46
Yam and Lentil Curry 47
Lemon Garlic Shrimp over Zoodles 48

Tuscan Shrimp with Rice..50

Skillet Ground Beef Stroganoff...52

Oven-Roasted Chicken and Broccoli in a Light Cream Sauce over Penne Pasta 53

Grilled Swordfish with Caper Sauce 55

Horseradish Encrusted Salmon..56

Sun-Dried Tomato Ravioli 57

Sides

Allie's Signature Mushroom Risotto..60

Red Beans and Rice..62

Creamy Orzo with Mushrooms..63

Coconut Rice..64

Roasted Acorn Squash..65

Couscous Patties...66

Moroccan Tagine Vegetables...67

Garlic Roasted Red Potatoes...68

Desserts

Cookies 'n' Creme Cookies 70

Peanut Butter Pie 71

Lemon Poppyseed Bundt Cake...73

Lemon Blueberry Cake..74

A Selection of Recipes from the Gourmet Cooking Club

Bastilla Recipe 76

Gourmet Club Dinner
(Chocolate Night)

Tamale Pie 82

Turkey Mole..85

Chocolate Amaretto Cigar Cookies 87

Gourmet Club Dinner
(Italian Night)

Beginnings 92

Intermediates 94

Side Dishes...97

Salads (Insalate)..98

Endings...99

Wine Pairing Recommendations

Cooking Charts

Seafood Cooking Chart...104

Steak Cooking Chart...105

Lamb Chops Cooking Charts...106

Home Chef Contributors' Profiles

Erin Fahey

My name is Erin Fahey, and I am a third-grade teacher in New Jersey. I enjoy baking in my free time, especially making cookies and cakes. I won my town's baking contest a few years ago and won a Yankees baking contest as well. I love that baking lets me be creative.

Tamar Matzkevich

Tamar, who grew up in Israel, started baking when she was seven years old, and a few years later started cooking dinners for her family. She experimented cooking many international cuisines, but her go-to when she's cooking at home is Mediterranean food. For desserts, she'll usually make her favorite chocolate mousse, and whatever she eats, she enjoys with a glass of red wine.

Kelsey Walter

I first started my adventures cooking in my suite in college. I would have my roommates taste test all my new creations. I have been cooking for about ten years, and I have been gradually perfecting some of my favorite recipes! My recipes range from Air frying-Zoodles. I am known to have too many kitchen gadgets, and love to share my cooking hacks and tricks. Check me out online: www.lqrecipes.com

Allison Mcnerney

Hello, everyone. I'm Allison, daughter number three of five of Lou. Cooking has always been my passion from a young age, and it followed me through life! I continued school and became a chef and worked in many different restaurants. However, restaurant life is not my passion. Although I find peace while cooking, I discovered that for me, cooking means family. Ever since I was young cooking in the kitchen, I was always surrounded by family and friends that I consider family. This dish is my number one request, so I decided to share it with you.

Mary Lavoie—US Army (Ret.) Veteran

I learned how to cook late in life, around my mid-thirties. It all began when I started hosting gatherings, mainly potlucks. I try to find new recipes based on that day's cravings, and I would put my own spin on everything. Hosting for all my friends is still one of my favorite pastimes, and my cooking skills have improved quite a bit since starting my culinary journey. I hope you enjoy these couple of recipes I have submitted to Lou (you are more than welcome to put your own spin on them as well).

Sedona Mcnerney

Hi, I'm Sedona, daughter number four! Most of my memories growing up are centered around the kitchen, as that was a place we gathered as a family and spent quality time together, whether it be cooking, baking, or sharing a meal around the table. Cooking has always been something I loved; I like to think of it as yet another art form, a way of expressing myself and my creativity. Making the decision to go vegan three years ago has only added to the fun of it all, and has encouraged me to be even more conscious of the food I eat, the resources required to produce them, and just how much love it takes to nourish our bodies. My absolute favorite part of cooking comes at the end, when you get to sit down and enjoy the meal you've prepared with your own hands, especially when it was prepared (and enjoyed) with the people you love most!

Kevin and Kristen Fahey

Kristen is daughter number two and is married to a wonderful man, Kevin. Kevin is the clever one who came up with the title "In Lou of Going Out" for my Facebook posts which inspired me to create this book. Kristen and Kevin love to watch sports together (Kevin is an awesome golfer who boasts three holes in one). When they entertain, they usually put out a host of finger food for the gang. They have included their game day appetizer—crock-pot buffalo chicken dip. Enjoy!

Rachel Griffith

Rachel is the owner and chef at Polkadot Dinners Catering in Sacramento, as well as a local cooking and recipe contest competitor. Chef Rachel has showcased her award-winning recipes at various Northern California fairs and festivals and has been featured on local Sacramento area news stations to showcase her award-winning and innovative recipes over twenty-five times.

Appetizers

Yield: 20 small spring rolls

Ingredients

1 egg
1 tablespoon fish sauce
1/4 teaspoon salt
1/2 teaspoon pepper
1 shallot, minced
1 garlic clove, minced
1 scallion, chopped
1/4 cup ground pork
1/4 cup minced shrimp
1/2 cup chopped mushrooms (pick your favorite)
1 carrot, shredded
2 ounces mung bean noodles (glass noodles), soaked in water
1 cup water
1 tablespoon sugar
20 rice paper wrappers
Vegetable oil, for deep-frying

Directions

Crack egg into a bowl. Add fish sauce, salt, pepper, shallot, garlic, and scallion, and mix well. Add pork and shrimp. Mix. Add mushrooms, carrot, and noodles, and mix together.

In a large pie plate or flat-bottomed bowl, add water and sugar and agitate to dissolve sugar. Place one rice paper wrapper into plate and allow it to soften in the water. Remove from water onto a clean kitchen towel.

Spoon some filling onto one third of the wrapper. Roll over once. Fold in top and bottom. Roll until you get to the end of the rice wrapper.

Heat oil in a wok or deep saucepan. Add spring rolls and fry until crisp.

Serve with sweet chili dipping sauce.

Game Day Appetizer
Crockpot Buffalo Chicken Dip
Submitted by Kristen and Kevin Fahey

Ingredients

1 bag of rotisserie chicken stripes (already cooked)
Ranch dressing
Frank's hot sauce
1 package of cream cheese
1 bag of shredded cheddar cheese
Tortilla chips for dipping

Directions

Place everything into the Crock-Pot with the cream cheese at the bottom, as much ranch dressing and hot sauce as you like, and then add chicken and the shredded cheese last so it's on top! Cook on high for about an hour, stirring occasionally.

Taste with tortilla chip.

Add any ranch or hot sauce if needed.

Switch the crockpot to keep warm and enjoy!

Avocado Cilantro Deviled Eggs
Home Chef Lou

Makes 12 deviled eggs

Ingredients

6 large eggs, hard-boiled and halved
1 1/2 avocados, peeled and diced
1/4 cup low-fat sour cream or mayonnaise
2 tablespoons cilantro
1/2 teaspoon black pepper
1/2 teaspoon salt
1/2 teaspoon celery salt
One lime, zested, use juice of 1/2
Cilantro, for garnish
Lime wedge, for garnish
Paprika, for garnish

Directions

Cut the hard-boiled eggs in half. Add the yolks to a blender and set the whites aside.

Add avocado to the blender, and mix.

Add in the sour cream or mayonnaise, cilantro, black pepper, salt, and celery salt.

Zest the lime and add the zest and juice from half the lime to the blender. Blend until smooth.

Fill a piping bag with the mixture and pipe a small amount into the center of each egg.

Garnish with cilantro, a lime wedge, and a sprinkle of paprika.

Spinach Balls
Submitted by Mary Lavoie

Ingredients

2 packages frozen chopped spinach
2 cups Pepperidge Farm stuffing mix
2 medium onions (chopped fine)
1 can water chestnuts (chopped fine)
3 eggs
3/4 cup melted butter
1/2 cup Parmesan cheese
1/2 teaspoon garlic powder
1/2 teaspoon thyme
Few dashes of Tabasco
Salt and pepper to taste

Directions:

Preheat oven to 350 degrees.

Cook spinach and drain.

Mix all ingredients (including the cooked spinach) in a bowl.

Shape into small balls (walnut-sized) and place on a nonstick cookie sheet.

Bake for 20 minutes.

Crab Quesadillas with Mango Salsa
Home Chef Lou

Ingredients

1 pound lump crabmeat
1 package of 6-inch round flour tortillas
1 medium green pepper, cut into thin strips
1 medium red pepper, cut into thin strips
1/2 of a red onion, cut into strips
1 tablespoon olive oil
8 ounces mascarpone cheese
1/4 teaspoon cayenne pepper
1/4 cup cilantro, finely chopped
1 cup Monterey Jack cheese, shredded

Cooking spray

Directions

Preheat the oven to 450 degrees.

Heat the olive oil in a frying pan. To that, add the onions and peppers. Cook for about 5 minutes or until onions are transparent.

Meanwhile, sift through the crab meat and remove any shell fragments. Stir into the crab the mascarpone cheese, cayenne pepper, and cilantro. Mix well.

Spray half of the tortillas with cooking spray. Lay them flat (sprayed side down) on baking sheets. Add equal portions of the crab meat and then equal portions of the onions and peppers. Sprinkle with the Monterey Jack cheese. Place the remaining tortillas on top and spray with cooking spray.

Bake for about 10 minutes or until golden in color.

After removing from the oven, allow to sit for a minute. Then, cut each tortilla into quarters. Serve with mango salsa (recipe follows).

Mango Salsa Recipe

   2 cups fresh mango, diced fine
   1 cup plum tomato, diced fine
   1/4 cup sweet red pepper, minced
   3 tablespoons fresh lime juice
   1 tablespoon fresh cilantro, chopped fine

Combine all ingredients together. Chill for at least 2 hours before serving.

Serve with hot crab quesadillas.

Artichoke Heart Dip

Submitted by Tamar Matzkevich

Ingredients

Mix together:
2 drained cans of quartered artichoke hearts
1 cup mayonnaise
1 chopped onion
1/2 cup shredded Parmesan cheese
Fresh ground black pepper (to taste; I use a lot)

Directions

Bake in 425 degrees for 40 minutes.

Serve on crostini rounds or any one of your favorite crackers.

Cajun Crab Cakes
Home Chef Lou

Ingredients

1 1/2 stalks celery heart, finely chopped
1/2 red bell pepper, finely chopped
1/2 medium white onion, finely chopped
2 bunches of scallion, green part only, finely chopped
2 teaspoons dried basil
1 tablespoon fresh oregano leaves, chopped
2 teaspoons fresh thyme leaves
Salt
Freshly ground black and white pepper
1/2 teaspoon dill weed
1/2 cup parsley leaves, finely chopped
3 cloves garlic, finely chopped
2 egg whites, beaten to stiff peaks
1 cup whipped cream
1/2 lemon, juiced
Hot sauce (recommended: Crystal's)
1 pound jumbo lump crabmeat
3 cups seasoned breadcrumbs
5 tablespoons corn or vegetable oil, for frying
2 tablespoons butter, for frying

Directions

Check the crabmeat for pieces of shell and put in a large clean bowl and immediately refrigerate until ready to use.

In a big heavy bottomed frying pan, sauté celery, peppers, onions, scallions in butter and oil. Add oregano, basil and thyme, salt, and white pepper. Lastly, add parsley and garlic and cook until soft. Leave to cool.

Whip cream in a large mixing bowl. Add dill and season with salt and white pepper. Add 1/2 of the lemon juice and blend gently with spoon. Add 1 tablespoon of the sautéed vegetables and herbs to the mousse. Fold egg whites into mousse.

Season with a handful of breadcrumbs, salt, pepper, hot sauce, and remaining lemon juice.

Fold in mousse, taking care not to overmix it. Fold in the rest of the vegetables and herbs and a handful of breadcrumbs. Blend it together very carefully with your hands, taking care not to break up any of the crabmeat and overwork the mousse. Gently work into little cakes and bread them with more breadcrumbs. Set aside.

Heat the butter and oil in a large heavy-bottomed frying pan. Fry the crab cakes until golden brown on each side. Only turn them once after the bottom side is browned.

Blonde Remoulade

1 cup mayonnaise (I used light mayo)
1 tablespoon red bell pepper, finely chopped
3 tablespoons green onion, finely chopped
1 garlic clove, finely chopped
1 1/2 tablespoons Creole mustard
1/2 teaspoon Creole seasoning
1 teaspoon capers, roughly chopped
3 tablespoons parsley leaves, finely chopped
1 teaspoon hot sauce (I used Crystal's)
1 teaspoon lemon juice

Finely chop all vegetable ingredients. Place in bowl and add remaining ingredients. Mix thoroughly, then refrigerate.

Olive Tapenade

Submitted by Steve Zeller

Ingredients

- 1/3 cup chopped pitted Kalamata olives or other brine-cured black olives
- 1/3 cup chopped pitted brine-cured green olives
- 2 tablespoons fresh lemon juice
- 2 tablespoons minced fresh parsley
- 2 medium cloves minced garlic
- 1– 2 tablespoons extra-virgin olive oil

Directions

Combine above ingredients, and serve with your favorite crackers or crostini.

Soups

Chilled Moroccan Tomato Soup
Home Chef Lou

Ingredients

2 medium tomatoes, diced (or 2 cans diced tomatoes)
1 stalk celery, minced
1 scallion finely chopped
1 quart chilled tomato juice
1/4 cup chilled orange juice (I used fresh-squeezed)

1 tablespoon olive oil
1 garlic clove, minced or pressed
1 teaspoon ground cumin
1/2 teaspoon paprika
1/4 teaspoon cinnamon

2–3 tablespoons fresh lemon juice
1 tablespoon cayenne pepper
Add Tabasco or your favorite hot sauce to taste

Directions

In a saucepan or a large refrigerator container, combine the tomatoes, celery, scallions, tomato juice, and orange juice.

In a small skillet on low heat, warm the olive oil. Sauté the garlic, cumin, paprika, and cinnamon for just a minute, being careful not to scorch them. Stir the spice mixture into the soup and add the lemon juice and Tabasco (or cayenne) to taste.

You may serve immediately or refrigerate.

Coconut Squash Soup

Home Chef Lou

Ingredients

1 whole butternut squash
Olive oil
1 can coconut cream
2 cups veggie stock
1 teaspoon cumin
1 teaspoon ground cardamom
1/2 teaspoon turmeric
1 teaspoon coriander
1 teaspoon ginger
Salt
Pepper
Bunch of fresh cilantro

Directions

Preheat oven to 375 degrees.

Slice butternut squash in half and drizzle with olive oil, salt, and pepper. Roast for 30 minutes until flesh is soft. Let cool.

Pour coconut cream into a pot set on medium heat. Add spices. Scrape flesh from cooked squash into the pot. Using immersion blender, blend ingredients until smooth. Slowly add veggie stock until thinned but still creamy.

Garnish with cilantro leaves. Serve warm or chilled.

Salads

Mandarin Superfoods Salad

Submitted by Rachel Griffith, Polkadot Dinners

Packed with SUPERFOODS, this AMAZING salad is sweet, a little spicy, and mostly…HEALTHY! But you won't be able to tell, and that's the best part!

Ingredients

- 3 cups prepared quinoa
- 1 cup chopped cauliflower
- 1 cup thinly sliced or shaved brussels sprouts
- 1 cup chopped walnuts
- 1/2 cup sunflower seeds
- 1/2 cup asparagus tips
- 1/2 cup diced red bell pepper
- 1/2 cup blueberries
- 1/4 cup dried cranberries
- 1/4 cup finely chopped green onion (whites and greens)
- 2 mandarin oranges, segments

Directions

Combine all ingredients and toss together with prepared honey-mandarin sauce.

Refrigerate, covered for 30 minutes, up to overnight.

Honey-Mandarin Sauce

- 1/4 cup honey
- 3 tablespoons Snow's Citrus Court citrus pepper oil
- 2 teaspoons crushed red pepper flakes
- Juice of 2–3 Mandarin oranges
- Juice of 1 lime
- Sprinkle of chia seeds

Combine all ingredients in blender and blend until thoroughly incorporated.

Pour over prepared mandarin superfoods salad.

Watermelon Goat Cheese Salad

Submitted by Rachel Griffith, Polkadot Dinners

Ingredients

1 small seedless watermelon
4 ounces chèvre cheese
2 finger limes
2 ounces whole pea shoots
1 tablespoon olive oil
Balsamic glaze
Flaked sea salt

Directions

Slice watermelon in half, then into quarters. Remove rind, then any seeds which may be visible. Cut into 1-inch cubes.

Form 1/2-inch round balls from the chèvre cheese by rolling a small portion in your hands until a ball is made.

Toss whole pea shoots in olive oil, then place on serving dish, lengthwise down the dish.

Place watermelon cubes on top of pea shoots, and then place Chèvre balls at random around the watermelon.

Drizzle dish with balsamic glaze, and add flaked sea salt, ensuring that each watermelon cube receives at least one flake.

Slice finger limes in half, then press out the "caviar" into a small dish. Use a spoon to disperse them at random on the dish.

Asparagus and Tomato Salad with Yogurt Dressing
Home Chef Lou

Ingredients

10 ounces asparagus tips and tender stems
1 tomato, chopped
2 tablespoons green onion, thinly sliced
3 tablespoons non-fat plain yogurt
1 tablespoon Parmesan cheese, grated (fresh is best)
1 teaspoon Dijon mustard
10 lettuce leaves

Directions

In a medium bowl, combine the asparagus, tomatoes, onions.

Set aside.

In a small bowl, whisk together the yogurt, cheese, and mustard.

Add to the vegetable mixture and toss until well-coated.

To serve, line salad plates with romaine lettuce leaves, and spoon salad on top.

Zesty Mediterranean Salad
Home Chef Lou

Ingredients

10 to 12 ounces fresh mushrooms, sliced
2 cans (13.75 ounces each) artichoke hearts, drained and quartered
1 can (15.5 ounces) chickpeas
1 pound of fresh broccoli florets
1/2 red onion, sliced very thin
16 ounces package of cheese tortellini
1 can (2.25 ounces) of sliced black olives
1 bottle (16 ounces) of sweet onion dressing or any oil and vinegar-based dressing you like
Parmesan cheese, grated (fresh is best)

Directions

1 to 2 days before serving:

Rinse the mushrooms and put in a bowl with a lid. Pour on approximately 1/3 of the bottle of dressing. Put the lid on the bowl and shake to coat the mushrooms. Place in the refrigerator and shake occasionally.

The night before serving:

Cook the tortellini according to the directions and rinse in cold water until they are cool.

Drain all the canned ingredients and place in the bowl with the mushrooms. Pour on the remaining dressing and toss. Sprinkle the grated Parmesan cheese on top.

If desired, serve on a bed of fresh romaine lettuce.

Pesto Orzo with Sun-Dried Tomato

Submitted by Sedona McNerney

Ingredients

1 cup orzo, boiled and prepared
1 veggie sausage, sliced
Several spoonfuls of sun-dried tomato
Pesto (see recipe below)
Sautéed mushrooms and onions

Directions

Prepare Orzo per box instructions.

Slice the veggie sausage and sear until cooked through, turning once in pan.

Slice mushrooms and onions and sauté for about 8 minutes until softened and slightly browned.

Combine all the ingredients in a single pan and add the sun-dried tomatoes.

Toss all ingredients together and mix with pesto.

Low-Budget Pesto Recipe

2 cups fresh basil (easy to grow your own!)
1/3 cup sunflower seeds
2 cloves fresh garlic
2 teaspoons of nutritional yeast
2 tablespoons of lemon juice
1/4 cup olive oil

Mix all ingredients in blender till smooth. Pour over orzo salad.

Breakfast

Easy Sausage Quiche

Submitted by Mary Lavoie

Ingredients

4 eggs
3/4 pound sausage, crumbled and thoroughly cooked
1 cup half-and-half or whole milk
1 1/2 cups of shredded sharp Cheddar cheese
1/2 small yellow onion, diced
1/2 teaspoon dry mustard
1 uncooked pie crust
Add salt and pepper to taste

Directions

Preheat oven to 400 degrees.

Roll out pie crust into pie pan.

Top pie crust with sausage, cheese, and onion. Or you can mix the sausage, cheese, and onion in a bowl and throw into the pie crust. Mix the eggs and half-and-half in a bowl and pour egg mixture over toppings in the pie crust.

Bake in preheated oven for 15 minutes. Then reduce heat, leaving the pie in the oven to 350 degrees and bake for an additional 35 minutes. When it is done, the top of the quiche will begin to turn a nice golden brown.

Remove and allow to sit for 5 to 10 minutes.

Sausage and Pepper Frittata
Home Chef Lou

Ingredients

1 tablespoon olive oil
8 ounces sweet Italian sausage, casings removed and broken into small pieces
1 medium red bell pepper, diced
1 small onion, diced
1 tablespoon chopped fresh rosemary
12 large eggs
1/3 cup heavy cream
1 cup shredded Italian blend cheese
Kosher salt and freshly ground black pepper

Directions

Preheat the oven to 300 degrees.

Heat the olive oil in a 10-inch oven-safe, nonstick skillet over medium-high heat. Add the sausage and cook, stirring occasionally and breaking up the pieces with a wooden spoon, until no longer pink in the middle and cooked through, 6 to 7 minutes. Use a slotted spoon to remove the sausage to a plate. Add the pepper and onion to the skillet and cook, stirring occasionally, until softened, 5 to 6 minutes. Stir in the rosemary and cook until just fragrant, about 1 minute.

Meanwhile, whisk the eggs, cream, cheese, 1 teaspoon salt, and a few grinds of black pepper together in a large bowl until combined. Remove the skillet from the heat and add the sausage. Pour the egg mixture on top and gently stir to incorporate the fillings. Bake until the eggs are just set and no longer jiggly in the middle, 50 to 55 minutes.

Let sit for 5 minutes before sliding the frittata out of the skillet onto a serving platter. Slice into wedges to serve.

Mains

Fusilli with Lemon Cream Sauce, Shrimp, and Spinach
Home Chef Lou

Ingredients

Extra-virgin olive oil
1 tablespoon minced garlic
2 cups heavy cream
3 lemons
1 bag baby spinach
1 pound large shrimp
1 pound fusilli pasta
1/2 cup grated Parmesan cheese
Salt and pepper to taste

Directions

Peel and devein shrimp. Toss in a bowl with a tablespoon of extra-virgin olive oil, salt and pepper. Grill shrimp on high heat till cooked through, 4 to 6 minutes, turning halfway through the process. Set aside. (You can either sauté or boil the shrimp if you don't want to fuss with the grill.)

Heat olive oil in a saucepan over medium heat, add garlic, cook for 2 minutes. Add heavy cream, the zest of 2 lemons, 2 teaspoons of salt, 1 teaspoon pepper. Bring to a boil, then lower heat and simmer for 10 to 12 minutes, until it starts to thicken.

Bring a large pot of water to a boil, add salt, and cook pasta according to instructions. About 12 to 15 minutes, stirring occasionally. Drain the pasta through a colander and return pasta back to the pot. Immediately add cream sauce and toss together. Fill a large pasta bowl with the spinach and pour the pasta and cream over the spinach. Add the shrimp. Toss until spinach is wilted. Season with salt and pepper to taste.

Serve immediately.
Wine pairings: Chardonnay, Pinot Grigio, Sauvignon Blanc

Pan-Seared Salmon with Lemon Butter Cream Sauce
Submitted by Donna McNerney

Ingredients

2 salmon fillet, pieces skin on
1 shallot or 2 small ones
Half lemon (juice)
3/4 cup white wine (dry)
3/4 cup heavy cream
1 hand full of fresh parsley leaves
1.5 ounces or 40 grams butter (3 tablespoons)
Salt and pepper
Olive oil

Directions

Get your vegetables ready, peel the shallots and chop very finely, the finer the better. Chop the washed parsley leaves finely (remove the stalks first if any and keep a couple sprigs for garnish).

On moderate heat, place a frying pan and melt the butter. Once the butter is melted, place the salmon pieces topside down (opposite side of the skin) and cook in the butter until lightly golden brown. Check underneath, and if light brown, flip over the fish (be gentle not to break them). Continue cooking until the butter is nutty brown.

Deglaze with white wine, add the juice of half a lemon, add the chopped shallots into the sauce, not over the fish. Add the cream. Season the sauce with salt and pepper. Keep poaching the fish in the sauce until cooked. This should only take approximately 3 minutes. It depends on the thickness of the fish and how you like it cooked. A touch translucent in the middle is perfect. If you like your fish cooked right through, maybe cook it for 5 minutes and baste it using a spoon.

Remove the fish carefully using an egg flipper or a fish spatula and place on a warm serving plate. Continue to reduce the sauce on high heat until it thickens to your liking. Add the parsley, mix well, and pour over fish.

Wine Pairing: Chardonnay
Sides: Garlic roasted potatoes (page 55) and steamed broccoli

Steamed Halibut in Lettuce Leaves
Home Chef Lou

Ingredients

    1 1/2 to 2 pounds skinless halibut fillet
    Salt and freshly ground white pepper
    1 large head Bibb lettuce
    1/4 cup very coarsely chopped fresh dill
    6 (4-inch) sprigs fresh mint

Sauce Ingredients

    4 tablespoons unsalted butter
    1 small shallot, finely chopped (about 3 tablespoons)
    1/2 teaspoon grated lemon zest
    2 tablespoons freshly squeezed lemon juice
    1/4 cup coarsely chopped fresh dill
    1/4 teaspoon salt
    Freshly ground white pepper

Garnish

    Small dill sprigs

Directions

Check the fish for any stray bones and cut off any dark flesh that was next to the skin. Cut the fillet into four equally sized square pieces. Season both sides of the fish with salt and pepper.

Separate the outer leaves from the head of lettuce without tearing them. Place a leaf on the counter-top, cupped side up, and center a piece of fish in the middle of the leaf. (If necessary, use two leaves to hold the fish.) Sprinkle the fish with 1 tablespoon of the dill and top with another 1 to 2 lettuce leaves, this time cupped side down, so that the fish is completely enclosed in lettuce. If needed, you can use toothpicks to hold the lettuce packets together. Wrap the remaining fillets in lettuce, sprinkling 1 tablespoon dill inside each one. Arrange packets, without crowding them, in a steamer rack or basket.

Bring several inches of water to a boil in the bottom of a steamer. Drop the mint sprigs in the boiling water and put the steamer rack or basket in place. Cover and steam fish 8 minutes for each inch of thickness (e.g. if fish is 3/4 inch thick, steam 6 minutes). While the fish is steaming, make the sauce (directions below).

After appropriate amount of time, turn off the heat, uncover the steamer and let the fish sit for 1 to 2 minutes. To check that the fish is done, carefully lift the top leaf from one of the packets and cut into the fillet. If the fillet is still translucent in the center, cover and steam for another 1 to 2 minutes.

Directions for the sauce

Melt 1 tablespoon of the butter in a small saucepan or skillet over medium-low heat. Add the shallots and cook, stirring, until softened but not browned (about 1 minute). Add the lemon zest and lemon juice and bring the mixture to a simmer. Vigorously whisk in the remaining butter, 1 tablespoon at a time, allowing each addition to melt before adding the next. The sauce should be slightly thickened, and the butter emulsified. Stir in the dill and season with the salt and pepper to taste.

Carefully transfer the fish packets to warm serving plates. Pour the sauce over and around the fish and garnish with the dill.

Wine Pairing: Pinot Grigio, Sauvignon Blanc

Rigatoni Bolognese
Home Chef Lou

Ingredients

Kosher salt
10 ounces rigatoni (about 3 cups)
2 tablespoons unsalted butter
1 small onion, finely diced
2 small carrots, finely diced
4 cloves garlic, minced
Kosher salt and freshly ground pepper
1 pound ground beef
2 tablespoons tomato paste
1/4 cup dry white wine
3 cups multicolored cherry tomatoes, halved
1/2 cup fresh basil, torn
2 tablespoons grated Parmesan cheese, plus more for topping

Directions

Bring a large pot of salted water to a boil. Add the pasta and cook as the label directs for al dente, about 12 minutes. Reserve 3/4 cup cooking water, then drain.

Meanwhile, melt the butter in a large skillet over medium-high heat. Add the onion, carrots, garlic, 1/4 teaspoon salt, and a few grinds of pepper. Cook, stirring occasionally, until softened, 6 to 8 minutes. Add the ground beef, 1/4 teaspoon salt, and a few grinds of pepper and cook, breaking up the meat, until no longer pink, about 4 minutes.

Add the tomato paste and cook until evenly combined, 1 minute. Add the wine and simmer until almost completely dry, 1 to 2 minutes. Add 1/2 cup of the reserved cooking water, the tomatoes, and half the basil. Bring to a boil, then reduce the heat to a simmer and cook until the tomatoes start to burst and the mixture is saucy, 4 to 7 minutes.

Add the cheese to the sauce, then add the rigatoni; season with salt and pepper and toss, adding more cooking water as needed to loosen. Divide among bowls and top with the remaining basil and more Parmesan.

Wine Pairing: Barbera, Sangiovese, Zinfindel
Sides: Garlic bread, green salad

Tandoori Chicken Skewers
Home Chef Lou

Yield: 6 skewers

Ingredients

Skewers

6 boneless, skinless chicken thighs

3/4 cup plain yogurt

2 teaspoons preminced ginger

1 garlic clove, minced

1 tablespoon (15 milliliters) garam masala

1 teaspoon ground coriander

1 teaspoon ground cumin

1/2 teaspoon cayenne pepper

1/2 teaspoon turmeric

1 teaspoon salt

Juice from 1 lemon

1 tablespoon vegetable oil, plus more for grilling

Directions

Preheat oven to 400 degrees.

If using wooden skewers, put in cold water to soak. Set aside.

Cut chicken thighs into 2-inch (5-centimeter) pieces.

Add yogurt, ginger, garlic, garam masala, coriander, cumin, cayenne pepper, turmeric, salt, lemon juice, and 1 tablespoon of vegetable oil to a large bowl and stir well to combine. Before placing on chicken, set aside some marinade to brush on after cooking.

Put chicken pieces in the bowl and stir to coat. Leave to marinate from a few minutes to a few hours.

Once chicken is marinated, remove skewers from water. Remove chicken pieces from marinade and thread them onto skewer.

Brush a grill pan with vegetable oil and heat over medium-high. Grill skewers until meat is cooked through, about 3 minutes each side. Transfer skewers to baking sheet and place in oven. Cook for 10 minutes.

Wine Pairing: Riesling, Sauvignon Blanc, Pinot Grigio
Serve over rice or couscous.

Grilled Hawaiian Style Chicken Skewers
Home Chef Lou

Ingredients

1/2 cup teriyaki sauce (the thick variety)
1 tablespoon minced fresh ginger
1 tablespoon brown sugar
1/2 teaspoon crushed red pepper flakes
3 cloves garlic, minced
Juice of 1/2 lime
Kosher salt
4 green onions, sliced
1 1/2 pounds chicken breast, cut into bite-size chunks
2 red bell peppers, cut into chunks the size of the chicken and pineapple
1 20-ounce can pineapple chunks, drained
Freshly ground black pepper
Olive oil, for the grill pan

Directions

Add the teriyaki sauce to a bowl and stir in the ginger, brown sugar, crushed red pepper, garlic, lime juice, a pinch of salt, and half of the green onions. Set aside.

Using wooden skewers that have been soaked in water for at least an hour, assemble your skewers.

Start with a piece of chicken, then add a piece of bell pepper and a piece pineapple, then repeat until you have 2 pieces of each on the skewer. Continue with the remaining ingredients for a total of 30 skewers. Season the skewers with salt and pepper and brush them with the marinade on one side.

Heat a grill pan over medium-high heat and brush with olive oil. Arrange the skewers on the grill sauce-side down (in batches if necessary) and grill for 3 minutes. While the skewers are cooking, brush the tops with the remaining marinade. After 3 minutes, flip and cook the other side for an additional 3 minutes.

Remove to a serving platter and garnish with the remaining green onions.

Wine Pairing: Chardonnay

Slow Roasted Chicken (Fall off the Bone Juicy)
Home Chef Lou

Ingredients

1 1/2 teaspoon packed light brown sugar
1 teaspoon paprika
1/2 teaspoon garlic powder
Kosher salt and freshly ground black pepper
8 bone-in, skin-on chicken thighs (about 3 pounds), patted completely dry
2 tablespoons chopped chives

Directions

Combine the sugar, paprika, garlic powder, 1 tablespoon salt, and 1/2 teaspoon black pepper in a large bowl. Toss the chicken in the spice mixture until coated. Arrange the chicken in a single layer in a flameproof 9-by-13-inch baking dish. Cover with foil and refrigerate for at least 4 hours and up to overnight.

When ready to eat:

Preheat the oven to 300 degrees.

Bake for 2 hours until the chicken is super moist and falling off the bone. Remove the baking dish from the oven and remove the foil. Use a spoon or ladle to remove as much liquid from the dish as possible and reserve. Turn the oven to broil.

Broil the chicken until the skin is golden brown and slightly crisp, about 5 minutes. Sprinkle the chicken with the chives and serve with the reserved pan juices.

Wine Pairing: Chardonnay

Sides: Garlic roasted potatoes (page 55), asparagus and tomato salad with yogurt dressing (page 17)

Roast Beef Tenderloin
Home Chef Lou

Ingredients

1 whole beef tenderloin (trim visible fat)
Kosher salt
2 teaspoons sugar
1/2 cup tricolor peppercorns (crushed)
1 stick butter
2 cloves garlic (crushed)

Directions

Preheat oven to 475 degrees.

Be sure meat is at room temperature (take out of refrigerator about 30 to 45 minutes before preparing).

Rub tenderloin with a generous portion of kosher salt mixed with sugar.

Press peppercorns on to surface of the meat. Cover as much area as you can.

Place meat on cooking rack in roasting pan.

Cook for 25 minutes for medium rare. (If using a meat thermometer, temperature should be 120 to 125 degrees.)

While meat is roasting, melt butter and blend in crushed garlic. Cook till it starts to brown.

Remove meat from oven and pour garlic butter over meat while hot.

Cover meat with loosely with foil wrap and let sit for 8 to 10 minutes.

Slice and serve.

Note: You can use the pan drippings to make a sauce by whisking in flour to the juices to desired thickness.

Wine Pairing: Cabernet Sauvignon, Merlot, Zinfandel, Syrah, Barbera, Sangiovese
Sides: Garlic roasted potatoes (page 55), zesty Mediterranean salad (page 18)

Lemon Spaghetti with Shrimp
Home Chef Lou

Ingredients

For the shrimp:
1 tablespoon extra-virgin olive oil
3/4 pound large shrimp, peeled and deveined
1/4 teaspoon kosher salt
1/8 teaspoon freshly ground black pepper

For the pasta:

1 pound spaghetti
1/2 teaspoon kosher salt, plus more for the pasta water
2/3 cup extra-virgin olive oil
2/3 cup grated Parmesan cheese, plus more for topping (optional)
1 tablespoon grated lemon zest (about 1 large lemon)
1/2 cup fresh lemon juice (about 2 large lemons)
1/4 teaspoon freshly ground black pepper
1/3 cup chopped fresh basil
2 tablespoons capers, fried

Directions

In a medium sauté pan, heat the olive oil over medium-high heat. Season the shrimp with the salt and pepper; add to the preheated pan in a single layer. Cook for 2 to 3 minutes per side, or until pink and cooked through. Set aside.

Cook the pasta in a large pot of boiling salted water until tender but still firm to the bite, stirring occasionally to prevent sticking, about 8 minutes. Drain, reserving 1 cup pasta water.

Meanwhile, whisk the olive oil, Parmesan, and lemon zest and juice in a large bowl to blend.

Toss the pasta with the lemon sauce, shrimp, and the reserved cooking liquid, adding it 1/4 cup at a time as needed to moisten. Season with the salt and pepper; stir in the basil. Garnish with the fried capers and more Parmesan, if desired.

Wine Pairing: Chardonnay, Pinot Grigio, Sauvignon Blanc
Serve with green salad, garlic bread

Yam and Lentil Curry

Submitted by Mary Lavoie

Ingredients

1 tablespoon olive oil
3 minced garlic
1 chopped onion
1 bar of yellow curry (I prefer the Golden Curry)
1 teaspoon grated ginger
1 seeded/chopped jalapeno
1 cup dried lentils
2 peeled and cubed yams
16 ounces chopped tomatoes
4 cups vegetable stock (or chicken stock)
Pinch of salt
Cilantro to garnish

Directions

Sauté garlic, onion, ginger, jalapeno in oil for 4 minutes.

Add lentils, yams, tomatoes, stock, and salt to boil.

Add curry.

Reduce heat and simmer for 30 minutes.

Serve and add cilantro if desired.

Wine Pairing: Riesling, Gewurztraminer

Lemon Garlic Shrimp over Zoodles

Submitted by Donna McNerney

Ingredients

2 medium zucchini
3/4 pound peeled and deveined shrimp
1 tablespoon of olive oil
Juice and zest of 1 lemon
3 cloves of minced garlic
Red pepper flakes (optional)
Salt and pepper to taste
1/2 cup chopped parsley

Directions

Spiralize zucchini. Set aside.

Add olive oil, lemon juice, and zest to a skillet. Once pan is warm, add shrimp. Cook shrimp for about 2 minutes per side until pink.

Add garlic and red pepper flake for an additional minute, stirring often.

Add zucchini and stir with tongs constantly for 2 to 3 minutes until slightly cooked and warmed up.

Season with salt and pepper and top with chopped parsley.

Serve immediately.

Wine Pairing: Chardonnay, Pinot Grigio, Sauvignon Blanc

Tuscan Shrimp with Rice
Home Chef Lou

Ingredients

- 1 cup rice
- 1 pound uncooked shrimp
- 2 cups heavy cream
- 1/4 cup parmesan
- 1 cup cherry tomatoes, halved
- 1 cup chopped spinach leaves
- 2 tablespoon butter
- 1/2 tablespoon garlic
- 1/8 cup chopped basil
- Salt and pepper
- 2 tablespoons of olive oil

Directions

Bring 1 1/2 cups of water to boil. Add 1 cup of rice and lower heat and cover. Cook until rice is tender, or until water has absorbed, about 15 minutes. Remove from heat and let rest for 10 minutes, then fluff with a fork.

As rice is resting, add butter and garlic to a saucepan. Cook until garlic turns a golden color.

Add cream and Parmesan, until sauce thickens. Add halved cherry tomatoes and chopped spinach. Once spinach has wilted, add shrimp.

Simmer shrimp in pan until cooked. About 5 minutes.

Season with salt and pepper and serve over rice.

Wine Pairing – Chardonnay
Can substitute rice with orzo or couscous.

Skillet Ground Beef Stroganoff
Home Chef Lou

Ingredients

1 pound ground beef

Kosher salt and freshly ground black pepper

1 10-ounce package white mushrooms, halved or quartered if large

1 tablespoon extra-virgin olive oil

1/2 teaspoon paprika

3 cloves garlic, finely chopped

1 carrot, cut into 1/4-inch dice

1 small onion, chopped

1 tablespoon tomato paste

1 15-ounce can low-sodium beef broth

1 tablespoon Worcestershire sauce

2 cups dried penne pasta

2 ounces cream cheese, at room temperature

1/4 cup sour cream

3 tablespoons chopped fresh chives

3 tablespoons chopped fresh parsley leaves

Directions

Heat a large nonstick skillet over medium-high heat. Add the beef, season with salt and pepper, and cook, breaking the beef into small pieces with a wooden spoon until well-browned, about 5 minutes. Transfer to a medium bowl, leaving behind any drippings, and reduce the heat to medium.

To the same skillet, add the mushrooms, season with salt, and cook until golden brown, 8 to 10 minutes. Transfer the cooked mushrooms to the bowl with the beef. Add the oil, paprika, garlic, carrot, and onion to the skillet and cook until the carrots are soft and the onion is lightly browned, about 10 minutes.

Stir in the tomato paste and cook until the tomato paste has toasted and is evenly coating the vegetables, 2 to 3 minutes. Add the broth, Worcestershire, and 1 1/2 cups of water to the skillet. Bring to a simmer and stir in the pasta. Cover and cook according to package directions until just al dente. Uncover, stir in the reserved beef and mushrooms, and cook until heated through. Remove from the heat and stir in the cream cheese, sour cream, chives, and parsley until the cream cheese melts and the sauce is creamy. Season with salt and pepper. Serve warm.

Wine Pairing: Cabernet Sauvignon, Merlot, Zinfandel, Syrah, Barbera, Sangiovese

Oven-Roasted Chicken and Broccoli in a Light Cream Sauce over Penne Pasta

Submitted by Kelsey Walter

Ingredients

- 2 4-ounce skinless chicken breasts, seasoned with garlic powder, chili powder, salt and pepper
- 8 ounces broccoli, cut in pieces, 1/2 inch thick, seasoned with garlic powder, chili powder, salt and pepper
- 2 tablespoons Caesar dressing
- 2 tablespoons ranch dressing
- 1/2 cup grated Parmesan
- 1/2 cup grated mozzarella
- 8 ounces penne pasta
- 6–8 ounces pasta water (reserved after cooking)

Directions

Heat oven to 375 degrees. Add preseasoned chicken and broccoli to a sheet pan or cast-iron pan. Begin making pasta, following directions on the box.

Cook chicken and broccoli for 8 minutes, then flip. Chicken and broccoli should be fully cooked in less than 15 minutes total. Cut into smaller pieces to add to sauce.

In a saucepan, combine 4 ounces of the reserved pasta water, Caesar and ranch dressings, and the Parmesan and mozzarella cheeses. Cook down and add additional pasta water until desired consistency. Add salt and pepper to taste.

In a large bowl, add pasta, chicken and broccoli, and sauce. Top with fresh parsley and parmesan.

Wine Pairing: Chardonnay
Sides: Garlic bread, steamed veggies

Grilled Swordfish with Caper Sauce
Home Chef Lou

Ingredients

2 swordfish fillets

2 tablespoons unsalted butter

2 teaspoons lemon juice

1 teaspoon shallot, finely diced

1 teaspoon minced garlic

1 cup white wine, divided

3/4 cup heavy whipping cream

1 1/2 tablespoon jarred capers

1 summer squash, bias cut

1 zucchini, bias cut

1 eggplant, bias cut

1 package herbed rice (long grain brown also works well)

Olive oil

Fresh ground black pepper and salt

Directions

Marinade the swordfish with 1 tablespoon of olive oil, lemon juice, and 2 tablespoons of white wine for up to 8 hours.

Preheat the grill.

In a heavy saucepan, melt the butter over medium heat. Sauté the shallots and garlic until lightly browned. Add the remaining white wine. Boil until liquid is reduced to half of original volume. Add the heavy whipping cream and stir constantly with a wooden spoon until volume is again reduced to half. Add the capers, lower the heat, and simmer for another 3 to 5 minutes. Remove sauce from heat.

Sprinkle the swordfish with fresh ground black pepper and salt and place on the grill. (Depending on the thickness, swordfish takes about 3 to 5 minutes per side.) Grill the swordfish until it just begins to take on a flaky texture.

Brush the vegetable slices with olive oil. Roast the vegetables on the grill with the swordfish until they are crisp-tender.

Prepare the rice according to package directions.

To plate: Make a bed of rice in the middle of the plate. Place the swordfish on the rice and drizzle with the sauce. Alternate the vegetables around the plate.

Serve with a nice Riesling wine.

Horseradish Encrusted Salmon
Home Chef Lou

Ingredients

- 4 salmon fillets (approximately 6 ounces each), skin removed
- 2 tablespoons flour
- 1 egg, lightly beaten
- 3 tablespoons prepared horseradish, divided in half
- 2 cups seasoned dry breadcrumbs
- 1/4 cup olive oil
- 1/3 cup light sour cream
- 1 tablespoon freshly chopped chives
- 1 tablespoon freshly chopped parsley

Directions

Lightly coat the salmon fillets in the flour. Place the egg, 1 tablespoon of the horseradish, and about a tablespoon of water in a shallow bowl and beat together. Dip the salmon into the mixture and then evenly coat in the breadcrumbs.

Heat the oil in a large frying pan. Cook the fillets for 3 minutes on each side, or until just tender and golden brown (the time will depend on the thickness of the fillets).

To make horseradish sauce: Mix together the remaining horseradish, sour cream, and herbs in a bowl. Serve the salmon with a dollop of the sauce on top.

Wine Pairing: Pinot Grigio (Chardonnay will not work because the spice will make it taste bitter)
Sides: Roasted baby potatoes sprinkled with fresh parsley and a crispy mixed leaf salad

Sun-Dried Tomato Ravioli
Home Chef Lou

Making homemade pasta is not nearly as difficult as you might imagine, and the difference in taste between fresh and packaged pasta is huge!

Makes approximately 50 to 60 ravioli

Ingredients

For the pasta:

2 cups flour (in a large bowl)	1 tablespoon olive oil
3 eggs	1/2 teaspoon salt

Directions

Make a well in the center of the bowl of flour. Mix the eggs, oil, and salt and pour into the well. Using your hand, slowly stir the flour into the egg mixture until a ball is formed.

You may need to add additional flour (if the dough is too sticky) or water (if the dough is too dry). The dough is the correct consistency when it holds its shape—without falling apart—but does not stick to you when you touch it. You should be able to roll it out with a rolling pin without it attaching itself to the pin.

Lightly knead the dough on a floured surface for about 5 minutes or until the dough is smooth and elastic. Divide the pasta in half and set aside one half, covering it with a moist towel. (You will make the ravioli in two batches so that the dough does not dry out while you are working with it.)

Roll out the other half of the dough, making it very thin. Cut the rolled dough into pieces about 2 inches wide by 4 inches long.

For the filling:

1 cup ricotta cheese	1 teaspoon each basil, oregano, and thyme
1/2 cup grated smoked cheese*	3 tablespoons finely chopped onion
3 ounces sun-dried tomatoes	2 tablespoons finely chopped green pepper

The variety of smoked cheese used will depend on your personal preference. You can also omit the smoked cheese and use more ricotta instead.

Directions

Bring a saucepan of water to a boil. Remove from the heat and add in the sun-dried tomatoes. Let sit for 5 minutes. Drain and finely chop the tomatoes.

To the tomatoes, add in the remaining filling ingredients. Mix well. Drop by the tablespoon onto one half of each of the dough pieces. (Do not use all the filling at this point because you still have another batch to make.) Fold the pieces over and seal by crimping with your fingers.

When finished with the first batch, go back and repeat with the second half of dough that has been set aside. Roll it out. Cut it in 2x4-inch pieces. Stuff and crimp.

To finish:

Additional ingredients: 4 cups of favorite tomato sauce and grated Parmesan cheese

Bring a large pot of salted water to a boil. Add in the ravioli and cook for 5 to 6 minutes or until tender. Drain.

Place 1 cup of your favorite marinara sauce in the bottom of a baking dish. Top with the cooked ravioli, followed by 3 more cups marinara sauce. Sprinkle with grated Parmesan.

Bake the ravioli in a covered dish at 350 degrees for 15 to 20 minutes or until heated through.

Wine Pairing: Cabernet Sauvignon, Merlot, Zinfandel, Syrah, Barbera, Sangiovese

Sides

Allie's Signature Mushroom Risotto

Submitted by Allison McNerney

Ingredients

Olive oil
3 garlic cloves
1 yellow onion
4 portobello mushrooms
Cremini mushrooms (one pint)
Shiitake mushrooms (one pint)
Fresh thyme
1/2 stick butter
1/4 cup red wine (optional; if you won't drink it, don't cook with it; white wine if preferred)
6–8 cup vegetable/mushroom/chicken stock (2 containers of store-bought)
1 1/2 cups arborio rice
Parmesan cheese
Salt and pepper to taste
Parsley for garnish

Directions

Begin your prep and smash the garlic and mince, chop your onions medium-dice, and whip clean mushrooms, and cut as desired. I like to cut my mushrooms in different sizes to create different textures (e.g., the shiitake can be sliced, cremini can be cut into 4, and the portobellos can be diced). Remember the stems of the mushrooms can be tough, so removing them is best and can be saved for making stock. The gills of the portobello is optional and can be cleaned out with a spoon. Lastly, the thyme you can remove from the stem and finely chop or add the whole sprig and remove before serving. Warm up your stock in a saucepan and set aside. Remember when cooking risotto, the rice will expand, so make sure you use a large enough pan to cook in. Also, the amount can change depending on how many are being served.

In a large sauté pan, coat the bottom of the pan with about 2 tablespoons of olive oil and 2 tablespoons of butter. Add in your chopped onions, followed by the garlic. Give it a mix and add in your mushrooms gradually. I suggest one kind at a time (shiitake mushrooms will soak up all the moisture in the pan, so add them last). If needed, add some butter. Add the thyme, salt, and pepper and let the mushrooms cook down. When the mushrooms are cooked down and there is still the juices from the mushrooms (you can remove some of the cooked mushrooms and save for a garnish before serving), add the arborio rice and allow the moisture to be absorbed and the rice to get toasted. When the pan is dry, pour in the red wine and pour yourself a glass too. Allow the red wine to be soaked in to the rice, stirring constantly, and then begin the risotto process. One-half a cup at a time, add in the stock that was set aside, and stir constantly until it is almost absorbed. Add a tablespoon of butter, repeating the process until the rice is fully cooked. Before finishing the adding of the stock, add in some Parmesan cheese, and taste to check the doneness of the rice and to taste if more salt and pepper is needed. If you added the whole sprig of thyme, remove before serving, and add back the reserved mushrooms. Sprinkle some parmesan cheese and parsley, and enjoy.

Red Beans and Rice

Garlic bread is perfect on the side. You can find Creole or Cajun seasoning in the spice section of most supermarkets.

Ingredients

- 2 tablespoons olive oil
- 1 pound fully cooked smoked sausage (such as hot links or kielbasa), sliced into 1/2-inch-thick rounds
- 1 onion, chopped
- 4 garlic cloves, chopped
- 3 14 1/2 to 16-ounce cans kidney beans
- 1 cup canned low-salt chicken broth
- 1 teaspoon Creole or Cajun seasoning or 1/2 teaspoon cayenne pepper
- 3 cups cooked rice

Directions

Heat olive oil in heavy large Dutch oven over medium heat. Add sausage, onion, and garlic and sauté until onion is brown, about 15 minutes. Mix in kidney beans with their juices, broth, and Creole seasoning.

Reduce heat to medium-low; cover and simmer until flavors are blended and mixture is very thick, stirring occasionally, about 45 minutes.

Divide cooked rice among large shallow soup bowls. Spoon bean mixture over rice and serve.

Creamy Orzo with Mushrooms

Ingredients

8 ounces cremini mushrooms, thinly sliced
3 tablespoons extra-virgin olive oil
Kosher salt and freshly ground pepper
1 large leek (white and light green parts only), sliced and rinsed
2 cloves garlic, minced
12 ounces orzo
3 cups milk
1 1/2 cups shredded Italian cheese blend (about 6 ounces)
1 5-ounce package baby spinach (about 8 cups)
Grated zest and juice of 1 lemon
2 tablespoons chopped fresh parsley

Directions

Preheat the oven to 425 degrees. Toss the mushrooms with 2 tablespoons olive oil, a pinch of salt, and a few grinds of pepper on a baking sheet.

Spread out in a single layer. Roast, stirring halfway through, until well-browned and crisp around the edges, about 25 minutes. Let cool for a few minutes, then scrape up with a spatula and transfer to a bowl.

Meanwhile, heat the remaining 1 tablespoon olive oil in a large pot or Dutch oven over medium-high heat. Add the leek and garlic, season with salt and pepper, and cook until the leek softens, about 2 minutes. Add the orzo, 2 cups water, the milk, 1 teaspoon salt, and a few grinds of pepper. Bring to a boil, stirring constantly. Reduce the heat to a simmer and cook, stirring occasionally, until the orzo is al dente, 5 to 7 minutes.

Remove from the heat and add the cheese, spinach, lemon juice, and 1 tablespoon parsley. Stir until the cheese melts and the spinach wilts; add a splash of water if the mixture is too thick. Season with salt and pepper.

Toss the mushrooms with the lemon zest and remaining 1 tablespoon parsley. Divide the orzo among bowls and top with the mushroom mixture.

Coconut Rice
In Home Chef Lou

Ingredients

1 can coconut milk
1 can water
1 can (use coconut milk can) filled with basmati rice
Butter

Basically, you are creating a 2 to 1 ratio of rice to liquid.

Directions

Preheat oven to 350 degrees.

Grease the lining of a 9 by 13 baking pan (Pyrex works well).

Pour coconut milk into pan. Add 1 can full of water.

Fill can with basmati rice. Pour into pan.

Cover with foil tightly—no opening air gaps.

Place in preheated oven and bake for 1 hour.

Serve immediately.

Some garnish suggestions: toasted coconut flakes, chopped pineapple, cilantro

Variations: add 1/2 teaspoon cumin, curry, and ginger for a Middle Eastern flavor profile

Roasted Acorn Squash
Home Chef Lou

Slice Acorn Squash into wedges about 2 inches wide.

Make the dressing.

Ingredients

> 1/4 cup honey
> 1/4 cup soy sauce
> Red pepper flakes

Directions

Mix together and brush on the wedges.

Cook wedges at 475 degrees for about 15 minutes.

Serve as a side dish.

Couscous Patties

Home Chef Lou

Ingredients

    1 box couscous
    2 cups water
    1/2 red bell pepper, diced
    1/2 green bell pepper, diced
    Saffron
    1 egg
    Sour cream
    Salt and pepper

Directions

Dice up red and green bell peppers into small pieces. Place in saucepan with a little water on low heat and cook till soft.

Add additional water. Bring to a boil. Add couscous. Remove from heat and cover. Allow to cool.

After cooled, add 1 egg to couscous mix and incorporate the egg into the mixture. Them for a small patty with a scoopful of the couscous mixture. Heal olive oil in a pan, place patty in pan, and sear till you get good crust on the outside. Flip the patty and sear the other side. Set aside on a paper towel to absorb some of the oil.

Sauce

Place small amount of saffron in a spoonful of hot water. Add 1/2 cup of sour cream. Sprinkle in small amounts of salt and pepper. Mix completely.

Moroccan Tagine Vegetables
Home Chef Lou

100% Vegan

Ingredients

1/2 dozen prunes, chopped
2 garlic cloves, chopped
1 small shallot, chopped
1 small onion, sliced thin
2 carrots chopped
1/2 eggplant, cut into 1/2-inch blocks
1/2 head cauliflower, roughly cut
2 tomatoes, diced
1 zucchini, 1/4 slices
1 teaspoon cumin
1 teaspoon ground cardamom
1 teaspoon turmeric
1 teaspoon coriander
2 cups veggie stock
1/2 cup toasted almonds

Directions

Traditionally, this is prepared in a tagine pot. If you don't have one, a Dutch oven pot will do.

The idea is to steam the ingredients in their own juices during the cooking process.

Place prunes in the pot over high heat and add 1 cup water. Bring to a simmer.

Add veggie stock and all the additional vegetables and spices. Simmer for 10 minutes.

In a separate pan, toast almonds till golden brown.

Assemble cooked vegetables in plate. Add almonds. Can be served alongside couscous or rice. Makes a great side for the Moroccan Tandoori Chicken Skewers on page 30.

Garlic Roasted Red Potatoes
Home Chef Lou

Ingredients

8-10 red potatoes
Garlic
Olive oil
Salt
Pepper
Parsley

Directions

Preheat oven to 400 degrees.

Slice potatoes in quarters (medium-sized pieces)

Mince garlic.

Mix in a bowl with olive oil, garlic, salt and pepper (to taste).

Place on an oiled baking sheet and roast for 30 minutes until potatoes are golden brown on the edges.

Transfer to serving bowl. Sprinkle with chopped parsley.

Serve hot.

Desserts

Cookies 'n' Creme Cookies

Submitted by Erin Fahey

Ingredients

1 cup of butter (2 sticks), softened

1/2 cup packed light brown sugar

1/2 cup white sugar

1 package of cookies 'n' creme pudding mix

2 eggs

1 teaspoon vanilla

2 1/4 cups flour

1 teaspoon salt

1 teaspoon baking soda

24 Oreo cookies hand-crushed or chopped

1 cup chocolate chunks

1/2 cup dark chocolate chips (white chocolate chips can be used if desired as well)

Directions

Preheat the oven to 350 degrees.

In a mixer, cream together the butter and both sugars.

Stir in the pudding mix (powder).

Add eggs and vanilla to cream the mixture.

Mix the flour, baking soda, and salt into the mixture.

Crush/chop the 24 Oreos and add to the mixture.

Add the chocolate chips to the mixture and stir well.

Drop spoonfuls onto a baking sheet (silicone mats work best).

Bake for 7 to 9 minutes until barely brown on top.

Note: they will look uncooked, but they are done!
Let them cool and enjoy!

Note: They can be made with different varieties/flavors of Oreos. For example, I also make them with the new Chocolate Peanut Butter Pie Oreos and put peanut butter chips in instead of chocolate ones. Feel free to get creative! All other ingredients remain the same. Just swap out the Oreo flavor and/or the chocolate chip flavor.

Peanut Butter Pie
Submitted by Erin Fahey

Ingredients

Oreo pie crust
1 bag of mini Reese's Peanut Butter Cups
Dark chocolate Godiva pudding mix
2 cups of milk
4 ounces of cream cheese, softened
1/2 cup of confectioners' sugar
1/2 container of peanut butter (preferably Reese's)
1 carton of Cool Whip, thawed

Directions

Make the pudding according to the directions on box. Once made, let settle in fridge for 30 minutes. Spread even layer over bottom of the pie crust. Let sit in fridge while you create the rest of the pie.

In mixer, mix cream cheese, powdered sugar, and peanut butter.

Fold in 1 cup of Cool Whip. Be sure to scrape the sides to fully mix.

Drop in some mini Reese's mini Peanut Butter Cups and mix again.

Spoon over the pudding mix. Spread evenly.

Spread remaining Cool Whip on top of peanut butter layer.

Use rest of Reese's mini Peanut Butter Cups to decorate top. Line edge with whole ones. Chop up the rest and spread in middle.

Let settle in fridge for a few hours before serving.

Lemon Poppyseed Bundt Cake
Home Chef Lou

Ingredients

Zest of 2 lemons

1 1/2 cups sugar

2 1/2 sticks butter

2 teaspoons vanilla

5 eggs

1/2 cup lemon juice

1 1/4 teaspoons baking powder

1/4 teaspoons baking soda

Pinch of salt

2 3/4 cups flour

1/4 cup poppy seeds

Icing

1/4 cup and 1 tablespoon lemon juice

1 cup confectioners' sugar

To make icing, combine confectioner's sugar and lemon juice in small bowl and stir until smooth.

Directions

Preheat oven to 325 degrees. Butter and flour Bundt pan.

Mix lemon zest with sugar in small bowl.

In a large bowl, beat together the butter and sugar with an electric mixer until light and fluffy.

Beat in vanilla and eggs one at a time.

Beat in lemon juice, baking powder, and soda and salt.

Mix in the flour until well-combined.

Stir in poppy seeds.

Pour the batter into prepared Bundt pan.

Bake at 325 degrees for 45 minutes or until a knife comes out clean.

Cool cake for fifteen minutes and then flip out of pan.

When cake has cooled, drizzle icing over cake and serve.

Lemon Blueberry Cake
Home Chef Lou

Makes 12 servings

Ingredients

2 lemons
3 eggs
1/3 cup (75 milliliters) vegetable oil
3/4 cup (175 milliliters) sour cream
1 teaspoon (5 milliliters) poppy seeds
1 package (15.25 ounces or 432 grams) yellow cake mix
Oil for brushing
1/2 cup (125 milliliters) fresh blueberries, plus additional for serving
Blueberry glaze
1 lemon
2 cups (500 milliliters) powdered sugar
1/4 cup (60 milliliters) blueberry jam

Directions

Juice the lemons into a medium bowl. Add the eggs, oil, sour cream, poppy seeds, and cake mix, and whisk until well-combined.

Brush baking pan with butter. Pour the batter baking pan, and top with the blueberries. Cook as per direction on the cake mix box.

After baking, let the cake stand for 10 minutes.

For the glaze, juice the remaining lemon into a medium bowl. Add the powdered sugar and jam and stir to combine.

Serve the glaze over slices of cake, and garnish slices with remaining fresh blueberries, if desired.

A Selection of Recipes from the Gourmet Cooking Club

Bastilla Recipe

This is a bit of a complicated recipe but well worth the effort. Your guests will certainly show their appreciation. I have made this dish a least a dozen times since 1998 and get requests all the time to host a dinner party serving this dish. This is a great brunch dish as well as a dinner.

Ingredients

- 1 whole large chicken, cut into pieces, skin and fat removed
- 2 large sweet white onions, chopped medium
- 1 tablespoon ginger
- 2 teaspoons salt
- 1 1/2 teaspoons white pepper
- 1 teaspoon black pepper
- 1 teaspoon turmeric (or 1/4 teaspoon Moroccan yellow colorant)
- 1 teaspoon saffron threads, crumbled
- 2 or 3 small pieces (2 to 3 inches) of cinnamon sticks
- 1/4 cup butter
- 1/4 cup olive oil
- 1/4 cup chopped fresh cilantro
- 8 eggs, beaten
- 2 cups whole blanched almonds
- Vegetable oil, for frying the almonds
- 1/2 cup powdered sugar
- 2 tablespoons orange flower water
- 1 tablespoon butter, softened
- 1/2 kilogram (about 1 pound) phyllo dough
- 1/2 cup butter, melted
- 1 egg yolk, beaten
- 1/2 cup powdered sugar
- 2 or 3 tablespoons cinnamon

Directions

Cook the Chicken (skip if you purchased a plain roasted chicken)

Mix the chicken with onion, spices, butter, and oil in a heavy-bottomed stockpot or Dutch oven. Cover, and cook over medium to medium-high heat, stirring occasionally, for about an hour, or until the chicken is very tender and falls off the bone. Do not add water, and be careful not to burn the chicken or the sauce as this will ruin the dish.

Transfer the cooked chicken to a plate and reduce the sauce in the pot until most of the liquids have evaporated and the onions form a mass in the oil. Stir occasionally and adjust the heat as necessary to prevent burning.

While the sauce is reducing and the chicken is still warm, pick the meat off the bones, breaking it into small 2-inch pieces. Stir in several spoonfuls of the onion mixture, cover the meat, and set aside.

Cook the Egg Stuffing

Transfer the remaining reduced onions and oil to a large nonstick skillet. Add the cilantro, and simmer for a minute or two. Add the beaten eggs, and cook as you would an omelet or scrambled eggs. Be patient, as it will take up to ten minutes for the eggs to set. Some oil separating from the eggs is okay. Set the egg stuffing aside.

Make the Almond Topping (I prefer to toast them, toss in olive oil, and set in the oven for 20 minutes or so at 350 degrees)

Heat 1/2 inch of vegetable oil in a skillet over medium heat for about five minutes, or until the oil is hot. Test the oil by dropping in an almond. If tiny bubbles rapidly rise around the almond within a few seconds, the oil is ready. If the oil boils and splatters immediately, it's too hot.

Fry the almonds in batches, stirring constantly, until golden brown.

As soon as the almonds are richly colored, transfer them to a tray lined with paper towels to drain and cool. Toasted almonds will continue to darken a bit after frying, so be careful not to burn them while they're in the oil. When the almonds have cooled completely, pulse them in a food processor until rough chopped. Put them in a mixing bowl, and mix in the powdered sugar, orange flower water, and tablespoon of butter. Set aside.

Assemble the Bastilla

Generously butter a 14-inch or larger round pan (a springform pan is excellent for this dish).

Brush melted butter on each sheet of phyllo dough as you work. If using phyllo, take care to keep it covered with plastic as you work since it dries out very quickly.

Using your pan as a guide, overlap 3 or 4 single layers of phyllo dough in a circular fashion, so that the inner halves of the pastry dough overlap in the center, and the excess dough drapes over the edges of the pan. (Remember to butter each layer of dough.)

Place two 12-inch buttered circles of phyllo in the center of the pan. This forms the bottom of the pie.

The first layer of filling is the almond mixture. Cover the bottom with a thin layer.

Then cover with the chicken filling, and distribute the egg stuffing over the chicken.

Repeat the process twice, finishing off with a layer of the almond mixture.

Fold the excess dough up and over the almonds to enclose the pie. Flatten and smooth any bulky areas.

Brush butter on the folded edges of dough, and top with three more overlapping layers of phyllo, brushing butter on each layer. Fold down the edges of dough, and carefully tuck them underneath the pie, molding and shaping the Bastilla as you go.

Use your hands to spread the egg yolk over the top and sides of the pie.

The Bastilla is now ready for baking. It can be covered in plastic and stored in the refrigerator for up to a day, or in the freezer for up to two months.

Bake the Bastilla

Preheat an oven to 350 degrees. Place the Bastilla in the middle of the oven, and bake for 30 to 40 minutes, or until deep golden brown. Note that a Bastilla placed into the oven directly from the freezer will take up to an hour to bake.

Garnish and Serve

Generously coat the Bastilla with sifted powdered sugar. Sift the cinnamon on top of the sugar, or use the cinnamon to decorate the top of the pie.

Serve immediately.

Gourmet Club Dinner

August 1, 2003

(Chocolate Night)

This evening, the couples were challenged to come up with recipes that included chocolate as a main ingredient. The selections were delicious, and the meal was fantastic. A lot of red wine was consumed during the evening. It was fun and we each gained a few pounds for sure.

Tamale Pie

Makes 8 servings

Ingredients

For chili

4 tablespoons vegetable oil

2 pounds boneless beef chuck or rump, cut into 1/2-inch cubes

1 large onion, chopped

2 large fresh jalapeño chiles, seeded if desired and finely chopped

4 garlic cloves, finely chopped

2 teaspoons unsweetened cocoa powder

1 teaspoon salt

3 tablespoons chili powder

1 teaspoon ground cumin

1/4 teaspoon ground allspice

1/4 teaspoon cayenne

1 28-ounce can crushed tomatoes in purée

1 10-ounce box frozen corn

1 1/2 cups water

1 15 to 16-ounce can pinto or black beans, rinsed and drained

1 cup chopped pimiento-stuffed green olives

1/3 cup chopped fresh cilantro

For topping

1 cup all-purpose flour

1 cup yellow cornmeal (not coarse)

3 ounces coarsely grated sharp Cheddar (3/4 cup)

1 1/2 tablespoons sugar

2 teaspoons baking powder

1/2 teaspoon salt

1/2 teaspoon ground cumin

1/4 cup finely chopped fresh cilantro

1 medium fresh jalapeño chile, seeded and finely chopped

3/4 cup milk

3 tablespoons unsalted butter, melted and cooled

1 large egg, lightly beaten

Directions

Make chili:

Heat 3 tablespoons oil in a 5 to 6-quart heavy pot over moderately high heat until hot but not smoking, then brown beef in 4 batches, stirring occasionally, about 4 minutes per batch, transferring with a slotted spoon to a bowl.

Add remaining tablespoon oil to pot and sauté onion and jalapeños over moderately high heat, stirring, until onion is softened, about 4 minutes. Reduce heat to moderate, then add garlic, cocoa powder, salt, and spices, and cook, stirring, 1 minute. Return beef to pot with any juices that have accumulated in bowl and stir in tomatoes, corn, and water. Simmer chili, uncovered, stirring occasionally, until meat is very tender, 1 1/4 to 1 1/2 hours.

Remove from heat and stir in beans, olives, cilantro, and salt to taste. Transfer chili to a shallow 3-quart baking dish.

Make topping:

Preheat oven to 400 degrees.

Whisk together flour, cornmeal, cheese, sugar, baking powder, salt, cumin, cilantro, and jalapeño in a large bowl.

Whisk together milk, butter, and egg in a small bowl, then stir into flour mixture until just combined.

Drop batter by large spoonfuls (about 8) over chili, spacing them evenly, and bake in middle of oven for 10 minutes. Reduce temperature to 350 degrees and bake pie until topping is cooked through, about 30 minutes more.

Cook's note: Chili can be made 1 day ahead and cooled, uncovered, then chilled, covered.

Turkey Mole

Makes 4 servings

Ingredients

  1 turkey breast and wing
  1 1/2 teaspoons salt
  2 medium onions, chopped
  Bacon fat or oil
  2 cloves garlic
  2 tablespoons chili powder
  1 small dried hot red chile powder
  1 cup ground nuts (almonds, walnuts, peanuts, or cashews)
  1 ounce bitter chocolate
  1 cup ripe olives (optional)

Directions

Cut the turkey wing into 2 pieces, and the breast into 3 or 4 pieces. Place in large kettle with enough water to cover, and bring to a boil. Add the salt, and simmer for 30 minutes. Meanwhile, brown the onion in bacon fat or oil. Add to kettle, along with garlic, chili powder, red pepper, nuts, and chocolate. Cover and simmer until turkey is tender and the sauce is well-blended and thickened. Correct seasoning. Add olives about ten minutes before serving, if you wish.

Serve with polenta and a cucumber salad.

Source: House and Garden 1965

Puréed ancho chilies lend a rich, sweet, and only mildly hot flavor to this chili. To make a hotter dish, do not remove the veins or seeds from the chilies. If anchos or similar dried chilies are not readily available, substitute one roasted and peeled red bell pepper and 1/4 teaspoon dried hot red pepper flakes when puréeing.

Ingredients

  2 dried ancho chilies
  1/4 cup cashews, raw or roasted

1 cup chicken broth

2 whole chicken legs plus 1/2 chicken breast (about 1 1/2 pounds total)

2 tablespoons olive oil

1 large onion, chopped coarse

3 garlic cloves, chopped fine

1 tablespoon ground cumin

1 teaspoon chili powder

1 teaspoon salt

3 tablespoons chopped fresh coriander sprigs (wash and dry before chopping)

14 1/2-ounce cans diced tomatoes with juice

1/2 cup cashews, raw or roasted

1/2 ounce fine-quality bittersweet chocolate (not unsweetened) or semisweet chocolate

1 cup canned kidney beans, rinsed and drained

Directions

Heat a small heavy skillet over moderate heat until hot, and toast chilies, 1 at a time, pressing down with tongs, a few seconds on each side to make more pliable. Wearing rubber gloves, seed and devein chilies. In a blender, purée chilies with cashews and broth until smooth.

Cut legs into drumsticks and thigh portions. Remove excess fat from chicken and pat chicken dry.

In a large heavy saucepan, heat oil over moderate heat until hot but not smoking, and cool onion and garlic, stirring, until softened. Add cumin, chili powder, and salt, and cook, stirring, 1 minute. Add chicken and stir to coat with onion mixture. Stir in chili purée, 2 tablespoons coriander, and tomatoes with juice and simmer, covered, stirring occasionally to avoid sticking, 45 minutes, or until chicken legs are cooked through.

Remove pan from heat and transfer chicken to a bowl. With 2 forks, shred meat. Discard bones and skin. Return chicken to pan and stir in cashews, remaining tablespoon coriander, chocolate, and beans. Cook chili over moderate heat, stirring, until heated through and chocolate is melted. Chili may be made 2 days ahead and cooled completely, uncovered, before being chilled, covered.

Source: Gourmet Magazine 1997

Chocolate Amaretto Cigar Cookies

Makes approximately 36 cookies

Ingredients

- 2 cups powdered sugar, sifted
- 1 1/4 cups all-purpose flour, sifted
- 1/8 teaspoon salt
- 1 vanilla bean, split and seeds scraped
- 10 tablespoons unsalted butter, melted and cooled
- 6 large egg whites, room temperature
- 1 tablespoon heavy cream
- 3 ounces bittersweet chocolate

Amaretto cream, recipe follows

Directions

Heat oven to 400 degrees. In a medium-sized bowl, using a wooden spoon, combine sugar, flour, and salt; make a well in the center. Stir to combine vanilla seeds and butter. Add vanilla, butter, egg whites, and cream. Mix until smooth. Cover and chill for at least 2 hours or overnight. Using the large hole of a box grater, grate chocolate. Gently fold half into batter, and reserve remaining chocolate in a small bowl.

Using a plastic lid, make a template by cutting a 4 1/2-inch circles. Using a small offset spatula, spread approximately 2 teaspoons of batter evenly to fill circle on parchment paper. Repeat process, making 3 more circles, and transfer parchment paper to a baking sheet.

Bake for 2 1/2 minutes, rotate pan, and continue baking for 2 1/2 minutes or until golden brown. Working quickly, use a spatula to remove cookies one by one from parchment paper, and roll around the handle of a wooden spoon, and cool on wire rack. If cookies harden before rolling, simply return tray to the oven for 30 seconds or until pliable.

Using a pastry bag, fitting with a 3/8-inch plain round pastry tip, fill with amaretto-flavored whipped cream. Gently pipe cream into 1 end of the cigar until cookie is full. Dip each end in remaining chocolate, and serve immediately. Unfilled cookies can be stored in an airtight container up to 3 days.

Amaretto Cream

Yield: 4 1/2 cups

> 1/4 cup amaretto
> 1 1/2 teaspoons instant hazelnut-flavored hot cocoa powder
> 2 1/2 cups heavy cream
> 1/4 cup powdered sugar

In the bowl of an electric mixer fitted with a whisk attachment, combine amaretto liqueur and cocoa powder. Stir to dissolve. Add cream and powdered sugar. Whisk on medium speed until soft peaks form. Refrigerate until ready to use. Follow piping instructions for Mocha Cigars.

Gourmet Club
Dinner

January 24, 2004

(Italian Night)

On this evening, gourmet members were challenged to find a favorite Italian dish. In traditional Italian style, we consumed an enormous amount of food and drank plenty of wine and spirits. It was a great evening.

Beginnings

Beverages (Bibite)

> A rose wine or Pinot Grigio (suggestions in wine section)

Appetizers (Antipasti)

> Melon (honeydew) pieces wrapped in prosciutto from Parma, Italy

First Courses (Primi Piatti)

> Risotto with Asparagus

Ingredients

> 8 ounces fresh asparagus, peeled
> 3 cups vegetable or beef stock, preferably homemade
> 5 tablespoons butter
> 1 small onion, finely chopped
> 2 cups medium-grain risotto rice, such as Arborio
> Salt and freshly ground black pepper
> 3/4 cup freshly grated Parmesan or Romano cheese

Directions

Bring a large pan of water to a boil. Add the asparagus. Bring the water back to a boil, and blanch for 5 minutes. Lift the asparagus out, reserving the cooking water. Rinse the asparagus under cold water. Drain. Cut the asparagus diagonally into 1 1/2-inch pieces. Keep the tip and next-highest sections separate from the stalk sections.

Place the vegetable or beef stock in a saucepan, measure out 3 3/4 cups of the asparagus cooking water, and add it to the stock. Heat the liquid to simmering, and keep it hot until it is needed.

Heat 2/3 of the butter in a large heavy frying pan or casserole. Add the onion and cook until it is soft and golden. Stir in all the asparagus except the top two sections. Cook for 2 to 3 minutes. Add the rice, mixing well to coat it with butter for 1 to 2 minutes.

IN LOU OF GOING OUT

Stir in half a ladleful of the hot liquid. Using a wooden spoon, stir constantly until the liquid has been absorbed or evaporated. Add another half ladleful of the liquid. And stir until it has been absorbed. Continue stirring and adding the liquid, a little at a time, for about 10 minutes.

Add the remaining asparagus sections and proceed as for step 4 of Risotto with Cheese.

Remove the risotto pan from the heat. Stir in the remaining butter and the Parmesan or Romano. Grind in a little black pepper, and taste again for salt. Serve at once.

Pork Stew
(Taken from *James McNair Cooks Italian*)

Makes 6 to 8 servings

Ingredients

3 pounds boneless pork, cut into 1-inch cubes
2 tablespoons all-purpose flour, preferably unbleached
1/4 cup olive oil, or more if needed
3 ounces Italian bacon (pancetta), chopped
2 cups chopped red onion
1 teaspoon minced or pressed garlic
1 cup dry red wine
1 cup Italian-style broth (see notes below), made from meat or chicken, or canned beef or chicken broth, preferably reduced-sodium type
4 cups peeled, seeded, drained, and chopped ripe or canned plum tomato
2 tablespoons tomato paste
1 tablespoon minced fresh sage, or 1 1/2 teaspoons crumbled dried sage
1 tablespoon minced fresh rosemary, or 1 1/2 teaspoons crumbled dried rosemary
Salt
Freshly ground black pepper
1 cup pitted Italian-style black olives, drained

Germolada

2 tablespoons minced fresh parsley, preferably flat-leaf type
1 teaspoon minced or pressed garlic
1 tablespoon minced or grated fresh lemon zest

Directions

Quickly rinse the pork under running cold water and pat dry with paper towel. Place the meat in a colander set over a bowl. Sprinkle with the flour, turning the meat to coat lightly and evenly with the flour. Shake the colander to remove excess flour.

94

In a heavy stew pot such as a Dutch oven, heat the olive oil over medium-high heat. Add as many of the pork pieces as will fit comfortably without crowding the pot, and brown on all sides. Using a slotted utensil or tongs, transfer the browned pork to a plate. Brown the remaining pork in the same manner, adding more oil as necessary to prevent sticking.

Add the *pancetta* and onion to the same pot in which the pork was browned, reduce the heat to medium and cook, stirring frequently, until the onion is golden, about 10 minutes. Add the garlic and cook for 1 minute longer. Stir in the wine and broth and scrape up any browned bits on the pan bottom. Return the pork to the pot, lower the heat, and simmer until the liquid has reduced by half, about 20 minutes.

Stir in the tomato, tomato paste, sage, rosemary, and salt and pepper to taste. Reduce the heat to low, cover tightly, and simmer, stirring occasionally, until the meat is tender, 1 to 1 1/2 hours. About 30 minutes before the stew is done, stir in the olives.

A few minutes before serving, make the *gremolada* by combining all the ingredients in a bowl.

To serve, ladle the stew into bowls or onto plates, sprinkle with the *germolada*, and serve immediately.

Notes:

If you decide to make the Italian-Style broth instead of purchasing canned broth, here's the recipe. Italian cooks prefer a lighter broth than the richer, more flavorful stock favored by the French.

Italian-style Broth

Makes 2 quarts

  2 pounds lean beef or veal meat; 4 to 5 pounds chicken, duck, turkey, or other poultry parts, including bony pieces such as necks, backs, and wings (do not add liver), or a combination of meat and poultry
  2 pounds beef or veal bones, if making meat broth
  1 yellow onion, quartered
  1 large carrot, peeled and cut into chunks
  2 celery stalks, cut into pieces
  5 or 6 fresh parsley sprigs, preferably flat-leaf type
  About 1 tablespoon salt

Quickly rinse the meat or poultry and the bones (if used) under cold running water. Place on cutting surface and cut off and discard excess fat.

In a large stockpot, combine the meat or poultry, bones (if used), onion, carrot, celery, and parsley sprigs. Add enough cold water to cover by about 2 inches. Place over medium heat and bring just to a boil. Reduce the heat to low, cover, and simmer until well-flavored, about 3 hours. Use a slotted utensil or wire skimmer to remove any foamy scum that rises to the surface; there will be more of this scum during the early stages of cooking. During the last hour of cooking, add salt to taste and remove the cover.

When done, remove from heat and let cool for a few minutes.

Line a colander or sieve with several layers of dampened cheesecloth, and place in a large bowl. Strain the slightly cooled broth through the colander into the bowl, pressing against the vegetables and meat to release all the liquid. Discard the bones, meat, vegetables, and herbs. Refrigerate the warm broth, uncovered, until cold, then cover tightly until well-chilled, preferably overnight.

When the broth is well-chilled, remove any fat that has solidified on the surface. Reheat the broth and use immediately, or cover and refrigerate for up to 4 days, or freeze for up to 6 months. Reheat to boiling before using.

Side Dishes

Plum Crostata

Prep: 20 minutes
Chill: 30 minutes
Bake: 25 minutes

Makes 6 Servings

Ingredients

1 1/4 cups all-purpose flour
1/4 teaspoon salt
1/2 cup cold butter (no substitutions), cut into small pieces
4 tablespoons ice water
6 tablespoons sugar
1 pound plums, cut into eights (about 3 cups)
1/2 teaspoon grated orange peel
1/4 teaspoon cinnamon
1 large egg yolk
1 tablespoon water

Directions

For the pastry, pulse flour, sugar, and salt in food processor to combine. Add butter and pulse until mixture resembles coarse crumbs. Add water and pulse just until mixture begins to hold together. Transfer to a board; shape into a ball, then flatten into a disk. Wrap and refrigerate for 30 minutes.

Heat oven to 425 degrees. Combine sugar and cornstarch in a cup. On a lightly floured surface, roll pastry to a 12-inch circle. Transfer circle onto a large cookie sheet lined with foil. Toss plums with sugar and cornstarch mixture, orange peel, and cinnamon. Arrange plum slices in center of pastry, leaving a 1 1/2-inch border. (Spoon any remaining sugar and cornstarch mixture over fruit, if necessary.) Beat egg yolk and water with a fork in another cup. Fold edge of pastry over plums; lightly brush pastry edge with egg-water mixture.

Bake crostata 25 to 30 minutes, until pastry is golden and fruit is bubbly. Cool on cookie sheet on wire rack for 5 minutes. Carefully loosen crostata from foil with large spatula. Remove foil and transfer to wire rack to cool. Serve warm or at room temperature.

Salads (Insalate)

Arugula and Pear Salad with Mascarpone and Toasted Walnuts

This salad was inspired by one we had in Rome that was made with Stracchino cheese, but we've used mascarpone, which makes an admirable and accessible substitute. (Stracchino, a springtime cheese, is difficult to find here, even in season.)

Active time: 25 minutes, start to finish

Makes 4 servings

Ingredients

2 tablespoons extra-virgin olive oil

3/4 cup walnuts (3 ounces),
    coarsely chopped

3/4 cup mascarpone cheese (6 ounces)

1/4 teaspoon black pepper

2 tablespoons fresh lemon juice

1 firm-ripe Bartlett pear

1/2 pound arugula, coarse stems discarded

Directions

Heat oil in a 10-inch heavy skillet over moderate heat until hot but not smoking. Then toast nuts, stirring until golden, about 2 minutes. Transfer nuts with a slotted spoon to paper towels to drain, then sprinkle with salt to taste.

Pour oil into a heatproof measuring cup.

Stir half of warm toasted walnuts into mascarpone along with 1/8 teaspoon each of salt and pepper.

Add oil in a slow stream to 1 1/2 tablespoons lemon juice in a bowl, whisking, then whisk in remaining 1/8 teaspoon each of salt and pepper. Cool dressing.

Halve pear lengthwise and remove core (preferably with a melon-ball cutter), then cut lengthwise into 1/4-inch-thick slices. Arrange slices on 4 plates, to one side, and drizzle with remaining 1.2 tablespoons lemon juice.

Toss arugula with enough dressing to coat and mound alongside pear. Spoon a dollop of mascarpone mixture onto each plate between salad and pear, and then sprinkle salads with remaining toasted walnuts.

Endings

Cheese (Formaggi)

Place a selection of cheeses on a platter including mozzarella, Pecorino, Romano, Asiago, provolone

Fruits and nuts (Frutte)

Add to the above platter olives, grapes, melon chunks, and some walnuts or pecans

Sweets (Dolci)

A selection of chocolate pieces including Ferrero Rocher, Perugina Baci, and Modica of Sicily

Beverages (Caffe E Liquori)

Serve a small cordial glass of either of these drinks: Marsala, Moscato, Frangelico, limoncello, espresso

Wine Pairing Recommendations

Beef and Lamb

Select red wine for beef and lamb dishes. Usually a full-bodied red such as a shiraz or cabernet/shiraz blend works well. Suitable wines include Barbera, Sangiovese, Cabernet Sauvignon, Merlot, Syrah, Pinot Noir, and Zinfandel.

Chicken

White wine is the usual pick. For grilled or roast chicken, try a Chardonnay.
For chicken cooked in a rich sauce, try a Shiraz or a medium-bodied Cabernet Sauvignon.

Fish and seafood

Select a white wine for fish and seafood. These wines would include Chardonnay, Riesling, Pinot Grigio, Sauvignon Blanc, and Gewürztraminer. Grilled firm-flesh fish matches well with Chardonnay or an aged Semillon, while a hearty stew is excellent accompanied by Pinot Noir. For flaky fish, choose a dry Riesling or a Chardonnay.

Spicy

Choose Riesling and sweet Gewürztraminer if your meal is spicy. The sweetness of these wines can be drank quickly to offset the spiciness of the food. Avoid adding a Chardonnay to spicy food as it will taste bitter.

Game

Choose a spicy red like Sangiovese or Shiraz for game such as venison or bison.

Tomato-based (acidic) meals

Serve Barbera, Sangiovese, or Zinfandel with tomato-based meals (e.g., spaghetti and pizza).

Duck, quail

Try a Pinot Noir or a Shiraz.

Cheese

Full-bodied wines go well with hard cheese, such as a full-bodied Shiraz with cheddar cheese. Soft cheese partners well with dry Riesling, Marsanne, or Viognier. Sweet wine is a good match for blue cheese.

Dessert

Sweet wines are a good choice, provided that the dessert is not as sweet as the wine.

Cooking Charts

Seafood Cooking Chart

For best results, thaw in the refrigerator before cooking (remove from plastic packaging). Cover seafood and refrigerate below 38 degrees. Once thawed, cook and consume within 1 to 2 days. Cooking times below are in minutes and based on fully thawed seafood. All times are approximate—cook fish or shellfish until opaque and internal temperature has reached 145 degrees.

Broil or Grill: Preheat broiler/grill. Brush the fish with melted butter/oil; season as desired.

Pan Sauté: Preheat 1 teaspoon of cooking oil per portion over high heat. Season as desired. Carefully place fish in pan. Refer to cooking times below as reference.

Bake: Preheat oven to 400 degrees. Brush the fish with melted butter/oil, and season as desired. Place fish on baking sheet. Refer to cooking times below.

	Pan Sauté		Grill		Broil		Poach	Oven
	med heat, covered		med-low heat, foil wrapped		low heat, uncovered		med-low heat	med heat, covered
	First Side	After Turning	First Side	After Turning	First Side	After Turning	Simmer	Bake 400 °F
Cobia, 6 oz.	4–5 min	4–5 min	4–5 min	4–5 min	4–5 min	4–5 min	8–10 min	15–17 min
Faroe Salmon 6 oz.	4–5 min	4–5 min	4–5 min	3–4 min	4–5 min	3–4 min	7–10 min	15–17 min
Grouper, 6 oz.	4–5 min	4–5 min	4–5 min	4–5 min	4–5 min	4–5 min	8–10 min	15–17 min
Halibut, 5 oz.	5–6 min	4–5 min	5–6 min	4–5 min	4–5 min	4–5 min	6–8 min	12–14 min
Icelandic Cod, 6 oz.	4–5 min	4–5 min	4–5 min	4–5 min	4–5 min	4–5 min	8–10 min	12–14 min
Mahi, 6 oz.	4–5 min	4–5 min	6–7 min	5–6 min	5–6 min	5–6 min	6–8 min	10–12 min
Sea Bass, 6 oz.	4–5 min	4–5 min	4–5 min	4–5 min	4–5 min	4–5 min	8–10 min	12–14 min
Snapper, 6 oz.	4–5 min	3–4 min	4–5 min	3–4 min	4–5 min	3–4 min	8–10 min	15–17 min
Scallops, US	2–3 min	2–3 min	3–4 min	3–4 min	2–3 min	2–3 min	5–6 min	12–14 min
Swordfish, 6 oz.	4–5 min	4–5 min	4–5 min	3–4 min	4–5 min	4–5 min	8–10 min	15–17 min
Wild Red Shrimp	2–3 min	2–3 min	2–3 min	2–3 min	2–3 min	2–3 min	3–4 min	6–8 min
Wild Salmon, 6 oz.	4–5 min	4–5 min	4–5 min	3–4 min	4–5 min	3–4 min	7–10 min	12–14 min
Yellowfin Tuna, 6 oz.	4–5 min	4–5 min	4–5 min	3–4 min	3–4 min	3–4 min	5–7 min	10–12 min

Steak Cooking Chart

For best results, remove the vacuum-sealed steaks from the box, and thaw overnight in your refrigerator. You can also thaw the sealed steaks in cold water for 30 to 45 minutes. After cooking, allow the steaks to rest 3 to 5 minutes before serving. Verify the degree of doneness by using your kitchen thermometer.

The cooking times below are in minutes and based on fully thawed steaks.

GRILL									
	Thickness	1/2"	3/4"	1"	1 1/4"	1 1/2"	1 3/4"	2"	2 1/4"
Rare 120–130 °F	First Side	2	4	5	5	6	7	8	8
	After Turning	2	2	3	4	4	5	6	7–8
Medium Rare 130–140 °F	First Side	3	4	5	6	7	8	9	10
	After Turning	2	3	4–5	5–6	5–6	6–7	7–8	8–9
Medium 140–150 °F	First Side	4	5	6	7	7	8	10	11
	After Turning	2	3	4–5	5–6	6–7	7–8	8–9	9–10
Well Done 160–170 °F	First Side	5	7	8	9	10	11	13	14
	After Turning	3	5	6–7	7–8	8–9	9–10	11–12	12–13

Gas Grill: Preheat grill to 450 degrees. Reduce to medium heat prior to cooking.
Charcoal Grill: Sear over red hot coals. For steaks over 1 1/4 inches, finish over indirect heat.
Tip: Download our easy steak cooking app!

SEAR ROAST							
	Thickness	1"	1 1/4"	1 1/2"	1 3/4"	2"	2 1/4"
Rare 120–130 °F	Side One (stove)	2–3	2–3	2–3	2–3	2–3	2–3
	Side Two (oven)	3–4	5–7	9–11	14–15	16–17	18–20
Medium Rare 130°-140 °F	Side One (stove)	2–3	2–3	2–3	2–3	2–3	2–3
	Side Two (oven)	5–6	9–11	13–16	18–19	20–22	22–24
Medium 140–150 °F	Side One (stove)	2–3	2–3	2–3	2–3	2–3	2–3
	Side Two (oven)	8–10	12–15	16–19	23–24	24–26	27–30
Well Done 160–170 °F	Side One (stove)	2–3	2–3	2–3	2–3	2–3	2–3
	Side Two (oven)	12–15	16–19	20–24	28–30	30–32	32–34

Sear Roasting: Preheat oven to 300 degrees. Heat a small amount of oil in a large ovenproof pan over high heat on your stovetop. Sear meat for 2 to 3 minutes on first side or until well-browned. Flip meat; then place pan in preheated oven.

Lamb Chops Cooking Charts

Grill or Broil: When charcoal broiling or oven broiling your chops, it's best to begin grilling or broiling lamb chops about 4 inches from the source of heat. Use a meat thermometer. Rare chops will register 120 to 130 degrees; medium-rare 130 to 140 degrees. Prepare one or two chops per serving.

	Thickness	1"	1 1/4"	1 1/2"	1 3/4"	2"	2 1/4"	2 1/2"
Rare 120–130 °F	First Side	6	6	7	9	11	13	14
	After Turning	3–4	4–5	5–6	6–7	7–11	8–9	10–12
Medium Rare 130–140 °F	First Side	6	7	8	11	13	14	16
	After Turning	4–5	5–6	6–7	8–9	9–10	10–12	11–14
Medium 140 150 °F	First Side	7	8	9	12	14	16	17
	After Turning	5–6	6–7	7–8	9–10	11–12	12–14	14–16
Well Done 160–170 °F	First Side	9	10	12	14	18	19	20
	After Turning	7–8	8–9	9–11	12–14	14–16	16–18	21–23

Sear Roasting: Preheat oven to 300 degrees. Heat a small amount of oil in a large ovenproof pan over high heat. Sear meat for 2 to 3 minutes on first side or until well-browned. Flip meat; then place in preheated oven.

	Thickness	1"	1 1/4"	1 1/2"	1 3/4"	2"	2 1/4"	2 1/2"
Rare 120–130 °F	First Side	2–3	2–3	2–3	2–3	2–3	2–3	2–3
	After Turning	3–4	5–7	9–11	14–15	16–17	18–21	22–25
Medium Rare 130–140 °F	First Side	2–3	2–3	2–3	2–3	2–3	2–3	2–3
	After Turning	5–6	9–11	13–16	18–19	20–22	22–25	26–30
Medium 140–150 °F	First Side	2–3	2–3	2–3	2–3	2–3	2–3	2–3
	After Turning	8–10	12–15	16–19	23–24	24–26	26–30	32–38
Well Done 160–170 °F	First Side	2–3	2–3	2–3	2–3	2–3	2–3	2–3
	After Turning	12–15	16–19	20–24	28–32	32–36	36–42	42–50

When the pandemic first broke out, home chef Lou McNerney took to the kitchen and started making home-cooked meals. One day he decided to post what he made, and immediately caught the attention of his followers. He responded by asking folks to post their meals and received great response. In conversation with his son-in-law, Kevin, it was suggested that he title his posts "In Lou of Going Out." Clever guy that Kevin.

After several weeks, folks were asking for recipes, and while in conversation with a close friend Amy, the book idea was born. Lou was inspired to publish a book of recipes and wanted to include recipes from friends and family. He wanted to contribute something positive to the pandemic nightmare we are all dealing with. Part of the proceeds of this book will be donated to Feeding America.

Lou is a longtime home chef and part-time bartender. He and his wife, Laurie, hosted a gourmet dinner club for over ten years from 1997 till 2007 in the Los Angeles and Sacramento areas. After the loss of his wife in 2007, Lou continued to host private dinner parties and share his culinary passion.

The recipes in this book are a collection of recipes Lou has created over the years, as well as recipes from family members and friends. Lou also included some of the gourmet dinner menus from the club's gatherings. He hopes you enjoy using this book to create your own memories.

Bon appétit!

CPSIA information can be obtained
at www.ICGtesting.com
Printed in the USA
BVHW060512130721
611805BV00002B/23

9 781637 106068